Vittorio Peri

Catherine of Siena

EDITRICE **VELAR**

On cover page:
St. Catherine in a fresco painted in 1460
by Lorenzo di Pietro called "il Vecchietta".
Hall of world map
in the Town Hall of Siena.

TEXT
Vittorio Peri

TRANSLATION
Sagayaraj Devadoss

FHOTOGRAPHY
Velar Archives

GRAPHICS
Augusto Maraffa

© 2006 Editrice VELAR
24020 Gorle, Bg
www.velar.it
ISBN 978-88-7135-259-6

Second Edition: November 2009
First reprint: September 2014

Presentation

At the time when there was little recognition given to women, Catherine of Siena emerged a protagonist.

She worked for the return of the Pope from Avignon to Rome in order to defend the Church, to promote a new crusade. She cared for the lepers and the plague-ridden. She was ambassador of peace between individuals, families and States. She consoled those condemned to death, counselled the popes and civic leaders. Disciple of an only Master, she became teacher of many disciples, particularly of a group of men and women who, from 1368, got together around her becoming her co-travellers on frequent journeys.

Whether her doctrine is recorded or her political experiences are recounted, some of the pages dictated by her are among the greatest literary pieces of the 13th century. And, for this, she is numbered as one of the great Christian writers and doctors of the Church.

However, Catherine was not just an intellectual or a mere professional theologian and not even a contemplative isolated from human history. She taught not from a pulpit, but at street corners, living intensively the events about which she was speaking and writing. When it was a question of announcing the truth, defending the Church, promoting peace, she was courageous and was not overcome by reverential fear for anyone.

Her words, like a double-edged sword, denounced intrigues and errors, no mater where it came from – even if they were from authoritative persons.

This book-let, besides being her life-sketch, is an invitation to reflect on her life and writings, although they are only briefly mentioned here due to lack of space.

The Autor

Essential Biographical Note

1347, 25 March**:** born at Siena, 24th child of Jacopo of Benincasa and of Lapa of Puccio of the Piagenti.

1353: First mystic vision.

1354: Consecration of virginity to Christ.

1359-1363: Strong pressures from her family so that Catherine could get married.

1363: She is received into the Third Order of Saint Dominic, made up of lay women called also "Sisters of the Penance or Mantellate".

1364-1366: She lives in a small room in her father's house, where she gives herself up to prayers and fasting.

1367, 2 March: Mystical Marriage with Christ the Lord.

1370: Change of heart (18 July); invisible stigmata (18 August). Catherine begins her service to the Church and civil society.

1372: For the peace of Italy she negotiates with the Cardinal D'Estaing and with Bernabò Visconti who is at war with Gregorio XI.

1374: First journey to Florence (May) where she is under the spiritual guidance of Raymond of Capua. On 29 June, she returns to Siena and assists those hit by the plague. Later she gets back to Montepulciano.

1375: First peace journey to Pisa where Catherine receives the stigmata on 1st April.

On the previous page: **Rome. Basilica of Saint Lawrence outside the walls.** *Saint Catherine (details) by Ludovico Seitz.*

Visit to the Carthusian nuns of Calci and the Gorgona (end of April) and again returns to Pisa (June). She writes to the captain Giovanni Hawkwood asking him to participate in the crusade. At Siena she works for the conversion of Niccolò of Tuldo. In September she goes to Lucca in order to invite the heads of the republic not to involve in antipapal alliance.

1376: She sends her first letter for Gregory XI in Avignon (France). She is sent by the magistrates of Florence, city under Interdict of the Pope, as their ambassador to Gregorio XI. She reaches Avignon on 18 June. On the 14 of August she says first of the 26 prayers recorded by her disciples. She leaves the city on the same day (13 September) when Gregorio XI begins his journey towards Rome. In Genoa (end of October) she exhorts the Pope to continue the journey. She reaches Pisa (November) where Lapa, her mother, awaits her.

Siena.
Basilica of Saint Dominic.

1377: Catherine founds a monastery for Dominican Sisters at Belcaro in the vicinity of Siena. She spends the last months at the Rocca d'Orcia and the abbey of Saint Antimo in an effort to bring reconciliation among various rivals. In December she returns to Siena.

1378: For the third time she returns to Florence (middle of January) where, during a popular tumult ("the tumult of the Ciompi") an attempt is made upon her life. For a short while (June-July) she retreats herself to Vallombrosa. Then she returns to Siena (August) where she completes the dictation of her "*Dialogue*", the book of her meditations and revelations. She is committed to defend the legitimacy of the election of the new pontiff Urban VI (happened on 8 April) and to lead the Church, divided by the great schism with the election of the antipope Clement VII (20 September), back to unity.

1379: In ecstasy (6 May) she dictates contemporarily four letters to be sent to powerful men in politics. She leaves for Rome (November) to help the Pope in the purification of the Church and in the fight against the schism.

1380: She dies in Rome (Sunday 29 April) in a house close to the church of Santa Maria above Minerva, wherein she is buried.

1461, 29 June: She is canonised by Pius II.

1628, 27 August: Urban VIII fixes the feast for the 30 of April.

1866, 13 April: Pius IX proclaims her as co-patroness of Rome, next to the principal patrons of Peter and Paul.

1939, 18 June: Pius XII declares her patron saint of Italy together with St. Francis of Assisi.

1943, 15 September: The same pontiff proclaims her co-patroness of the Italian nurses.

1970, 4 October: Paul VI bestows on her the title "Doctor of the Church".

1999, 1 October: John Paul II makes Catherine of Siena, Bridget of Sweden and Teresa Benedicta of the Cross (Edith Stein) patron Saints of Europe.

Siena.
Gaia Fountain, in the Piazza del Campo.

Bibliographical Sources

Siena.
House of Saint Catherine.

In the following page:
Details of a letter of Catherine written to Neri of Landoccio in 1379.

Information on the life of Catherine of Siena comes fundamentally from two groups of documents: her writings – *Letters, Dialogue, Prayers* – dictated by her mainly in a state of ecstasy, and the biographies written by her disciples: *Legenda maior, Legenda minor, Supplementum, Miracoli, Processo Castellano.*

The *Letters,* collected immediately after her death and till today, are 381. Only some of them were written by herself towards the end of her life, while the others were dictated. Some of their peculiar aspects are the following:

– ***starting****:* beginning of the letters are always in the same style: *in the name of Jesus Christ crucified and of sweet Mary;*

– ***appellation****: father, brother, sister* were the titles with which the addressees were called;

– ***address****: I Catherine, the servant and slave of all servants of Jesus Christ, write to you, in the Precious Blood of the Son of God;*

– ***concluding formula****: I say no more. Remain in the holy and sweet grace of God;*

– ***invariable close****: sweet Jesus, Jesus love.*

The *Dialogue* – also called as "Treatise on Divine Providence" and "Book of the Divine Doctrine" by her disciples, and simply as the *Book* by Catherine – began its origin at Rocca di Tentennano in Val d'Orcia in the month of December 1377 and was completed in Siena, in 1378.

The 26 *Prayers* were pronounced and

...rissimo ⁊ dolcissimo figliuolo in xº dolcissimo ⁊ Jo caterina schiava de servi...
...oso sangue suo / co desiderio di vederev... cresco diuno ⁊ bassissimo
...re pacifico doue tu nõ auras dubitare... desse mar segata di dio / p...
...ba che operi... allo che sara rimasta alla tra ⁊aurale renduta e...
...luolo che iuene che viui i questa vita tu tingegni di viu... noso ad...
... vsionoso viuendo dara... a laloca... lauira
...ni che dio vuerri i te glla che pmisseq... ltro ne aurra sena p
...a tua via i pata dame et dallaltra aggariue. Cõfortati steti a
...delle suo mali nõ ne sarebbe tolto veruno / dico delle due parti p
...tu miveteadi singa molte parole. Vi spõdoti alla lette che me vi dasti...
...rtini sicome tu m scenn dio retibuista ibisfatori auita essa che...
...dõ alla nicciu... Jl inteso glla che mi scen delnorto / credo se alan...
...rebbe ame che diglli che visono cioe lebbare bysolo pra limte a...
...possono uced che frucio ursi faria et egli si possa venire nesse...
...bbo et alsuo vitello elquale e co lui et para che plorome desima...
...e vedono che sisafaresse dellandare asiena ti rispodo ch... gua...
...a veruna... per se tu vedi che si viua come decte e g... rispo...
...si feue uiti... tio che tu nõ vada ne ti pare...
...llo collicate uever i quato queste cose nõ aiustesthino / si tu cõ...
...bare bysolo... perche tu ai spatrato asiena ⁊ tu tene viei subbu...
...ome tu se ue... sa che tu mi scen. Ott. sopto altre lecte lequali...
...rispostoti adozi bisogno / et anco vedissi atomasino vna grade l...
...nforsti ⁊ scen a francesthello vna buona lette. dio le sara arriu...
...mi ramieta che iu abbi asstien ouero a rispond vn dimura cosa
...che forse nõ a ututa la lecte plaquale di che mi scen queste cose da
...scouo libbare tomasino francesthello ⁊ la dona dimisse ceccolo
...ziale bnsfacitu. sauona nicosesta ⁊ tucta laltra famigia, e il
...modo abiano buone nouelle che egli sia bn ⁊ lauosa molto fort
...la puuica di genoua ⁊ tosto sam fucto maestre i theologia. da sie...
...o aueuo licita dimurare belcaro / cpe me uedessi dicosta pote o
...si elfu. Apiamo tolta una casa presso asco biagio tra capo di
...tornare inanzi pasqua plagrā di dio. pmane nella sca ⁊ dolce
...ore. Facta adi iij di dicembre 1379

Jo p bernardo colnago bolano di calauia della compagnie di st...
scrisseno... questa lettera della gloriosa vergine s. cate
Domenicadei... posto a hesa padri predicatori...
... in questo pistesso di nano ne... pypria so... mo...
sau scritto il... proprio nome... il di 14 di...
℞ P. Bernardu colnagi el bolana ℞

The Dominican monk Raymond of Capua in the act of writing the biography of the Saint. From a xylography of the 1500.

immediately put into writing by her disciples.

The second series of sources of Catherine is formed by ancient biographies.

The most important is the *Legenda maior* which will be often mentioned in the pages that follow. Friar Raymond of Capua, who wrote it in Latin, was concerned about giving details of where and how he had collected information and abouth indicating the names of testimonies. At that time, all were still alive.

In order to help spread the document, the Siennese Friar Thomas of Anthony Nacci, called Caffarini, made a synthesis of it, which became known as *Legenda minor*.

This was later translated into Italian by Stefano Maconi.

Caffarini, who had gathered further information, wanted also to compile a *Supplement* to the work of Friar Raymond, focusing particularly on the incident of stigmatisation.

The Miracles of Catherine of Jacopo from Siena is the first biographical document on the saint written by an anonymous Florentine.

The "Process" of Venice celebrated between 1411 and 1416 (called also *Processo Castellano* for the fact that the city was belonging to the diocese of Castello) constitutes another valuable source of history.

Infancy and Adolescence

On 25 March 1347 in Siena, Monna Lapa of Puccio of the Piagenti, wife of Jacopo of Benincasa, a wool-dyer in Via Fonte Branda, gave birth to twins, Catherine and Giovanna, thus bringing the number of their children to twenty-four.

Jacopo *"was an honest, God-fearing man without vice"*, writes the biographer Friar Raymond. Instead, the energetic Lapa, quite different from mild Jacopo, was *"like an industrious bee who knew about the activities of the house and of the family"*.

The first significant episode in the life of Catherine happened in the year 1353. While returning home along with her brother Stephen after a visit to her sister Bonaventura, she saw on the roof-top of the Church of Saint Dominic, which she would have assiduously frequented, a beautiful throne on which the Lord Jesus was seated.

Some time later, Catherine had a room in her father's house all for herself. It was a quasi 'domestic desert' in which she retreated herself to pray. But the privilege came to an end shortly on the day when their family members saw her shaven-head. They prohibited her from staying alone and compelled her to do hard domestic jobs. Having lost the walled-room, she found refugee in that of soul which she called as privileged place for *"knowing oneself and God"*, *"deep-well"*, *"temple"* or *"cenacle where the Holy Spirit is received"*.

In that time, Catherine had a decisive dream in which she saw many founder-

Siena. Casa di S. Caterina.
La tradizione vuole che Caterina si appartasse per la preghiera e le penitenze in questo cubiculum. Nella vetrinetta sono custodite alcune reliquie.

saints of the Religious Orders. Among these she recognised Dominic of Guzman (1170-1221) who, showing the habit of the Sisters of Penance, invited her to enter his Religious Order.

The apparition forced Catherine to act swiftly. *"You know"*, she told her family members, *"that I have made the vow of virginity to my Lord. I should obey God more than the human persons. My Spouse is so rich and strong that He will not let me die of hunger"*. At such a determination, her father ordered the entire family not to hinder any more the choices of her loving daughter.

Besides fasting and keeping herself awake at night, Catherine wore also a coarse girdle which she removed only during her final illness. Lapa, not renouncing efforts to dissuade her daughter from plans, wanted to take Catherine along with her to the near by thermal baths of Bagno Vignoni.

But even in the warm waters of the baths, Catherine found ways to do penance, remaining always faithful to herself.

Bagno Vignoni.
The thermal baths of Bagno Vignoni, in Val d'Orcia, were very much appreciated. Even Lorenzo de' Medici, called the Great, went to these baths for the cure of arthritis.

Siena. Piazza del Campo.
It is situated in the place where the backbones of the three hills branch off. And on these hills is seen the city.

Catherine a Dominican Tertiary at last!

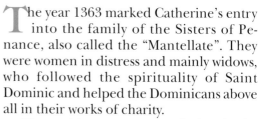

Siena.
*Church of
Saint Dominic.*

The year 1363 marked Catherine's entry into the family of the Sisters of Penance, also called the "Mantellate". They were women in distress and mainly widows, who followed the spirituality of Saint Dominic and helped the Dominicans above all in their works of charity.

The vestition ceremony took place in the Cappella delle Volte in Saint Dominic. Catherine received the awaited habit with the colours of her Siena: white veil and tunic and a black mantel. Entering among the Tertiaries, she gave herself to God also publicly. Not being a nun, she continued to live in her home.

The immediate successive period (1364-1366) marked a chain of mystical experiences for Catherine, but they were real meetings with the Lord who spoke to her and whose words she would have never forgotten: *"Daughter, do you know who you are and who I am? If you know these two things, you will be blessed. You are what you are not; instead I am what I am. If you have in your soul such recognition, then, the enemy will not be able to cheat you"*. She called the enemy, "Malatasca", the 'prince of darkness' because "mal sacco delle anime". The enemy never let her in peace for he insinuated doubts about the value of Catherine's choices and penance. To make the situation worse, there were long moments of silence from the part of her Spouse.

In a letter written to Bartolomea della Seta, a nun in the monastery of Saint

Stefano at Pisa, Catherine confided how she had rebuked the Lord and how the Lord replied her: "*O sweet and good Jesus, where were you when my soul was in such affliction? I was beside you. For I move not, and never leave my creature, unless the creature leaves me*".

From that moment onwards the meetings with the Master were becoming more frequent and familiar. He used to call her, "*my dearest daughter Catherine*", and to appear to her at times accompanied by the Virgin Mary or by other Saints.

On Shrove Tuesday, 2 March 1367, final day of carnival, Catherine celebrated the mystical marriage with her Lord. Many times she heard his mysterious promise: "*For my sake you have thrown away the vanity of the world and have chosen me. I will celebrate the solemn marriage feast with your soul. I shall betroth you to myself in faith*". The Virgin Mary, the evangelist John, the apostle Paul, Saint Dominic and the prophet Da-

Siena. Via del Costone. *While going down this slope, from the opposite side to the Basilica of Saint Dominic, Catherine had the first apparition of Christ.*

vid appeared to the twenty-year old girl of Fonte Branda.

The Virgin Mary invited Catherine to move closer to Jesus who told her the following: "*I marry you in faith which you will conserve spotless until you will reach heaven to celebrate the eternal marriage. From now on, o dearest daughter, do things with a strong-mind and without any hesitation.*" In addition, he gave a clear indication to live the Christian love in an authentic way: "*You know that there are two precepts of love: to love me and to love one's neighbour. I want that you follow these two commandments. You should walk not with one, but with two legs, and to fly with two wings*".

Catherine, then, began to go out of her house more frequently: initially to visit the poor and the sick; later on, to meet with people of every segment of the society, living in the magnificent palaces of the powerful and in the miserable prisons. After twenty years of pure contemplation, she began an intensive social and political activity.

Nurse and Teacher

The episodes narrated by the biographer on the dedication of Catherine, shown towards the poor, are indeed numerous. The episode of "crocetta" happened in the church of Saint Dominic when, not having anything to offer to a mendicant asking for alms, she gave him a small silver cross. The following night the Lord appeared to her with the same cross in hand, but fully studded with precious gems.

Another time, near the Chapel of the Tertiaries, a young man, covered with torn clothes and shivering with cold, asked her something to cover himself. Catherine withdrew herself, removed the tunic and brought it to the poor man. The following night the Lord appeared to her looking like the mendicant. He brought the same thing in hand what she had given to the beggar.

Besides, with concern she dedicated herself to many more sick people of the city, like lepers, and others who really needed cure. Every day, for instance, she used to visit a sick lady, called Cecca, in order to make her condition less inhuman. But the more concern Catherine showed, the angrier Cecca became. Although Monna Lapa allowed her daughter to visit frequently the leper hospital, she did not hesitate scolding Catherine: "*You will pick-up the leprosy yourself*". The sickness did come, and her hands showed the horrible signs of it until the moment of the burial of Cecca.

It was during this time that she obtained from the Lord the gift of being

Siena. Hospital of Santa Maria della Scala. *Saint Catherine in a fresco conserved in the very old part of the antique hospital.*

able to read the hearts of those who came to her and to know their state of souls. At times she was captured by the introspection of people that she seemed to have been lost not knowing what was happening around her.

Starting from the year 1368 a group of spiritual disciples started to gather around Catherine which she loved to define as "*nice company*" or "*poor family of the sweet Truth*". Instead, others called them, with some irony, as *caterinati*. Among the followers

Catherine offers the mantle to a mendicant.

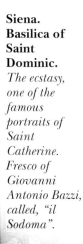

there were women and men, politicians and artists, noble persons and commoners, lay people, priests and religious who acted as secretaries or clerks and followed her in her mission of peace. One of the *caterinati* was also the painter Andrea Vanni, whose portrait of Catherine can still be seen in the Church of Saint Dominic in Siena.

On 18 July 1370 once again in the Cappella della Volte, Catherine was protagonist in a new extraordinary episode. She saw Jesus who showed her a throbbing heart in his hand. A month later, on 18 August, she was conformed to Him through an acute pain in the palm of her hand, a pain similar to the one when nail is pierced into one's body. From that moment on, that sign, although invisible, remained in her right hand like a wedding ring.

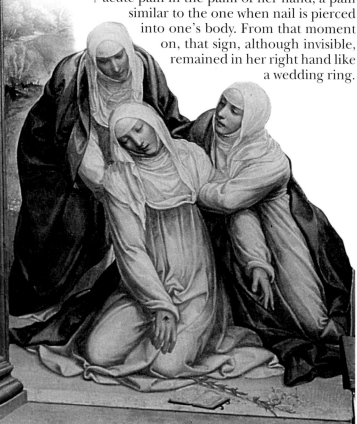

Pilgrim of Peace

Catherine gave significant attention for the life of politics because it directly involved the Church and, by implication the great interests of the people of God.

This way the 381 wonderful letters came to be born. The first ones were written to papal nuncio Cardinal Pietro d'Estaing, to Bernabò Visconti lord of Milan who was searching for a dialogue with Pope Gregory XI and to Beatrice della Scala, wife of the same Visconti.

From 1374 onwards Catherine ventured into a series of journeys as facilitator of peace between the Pope and the various cities that were constantly at war with the Pontifical State.

In May of the same year a General Chapter of the Dominicans was convoked in Florence in order to clarify certain aspects of Catherine's theological doctrines about which there were conflicting views emerging. It was here that she met Friar Raymond of Capua whom the General Chapter asked to replace Friar Thomas della Fonte as her spiritual director. During this short stay in Florence, she came to know about Niccolò Soderini, gonfalonier of justice and prior of arts, who later became her faithful disciple for the rest of life.

Leaving Florence, she returned to Siena which was devastated by a new bubonic epidemic. There was not a house or a street which did not witness Catherine taking care of the repulsive plague-ridden people, so much so at the *Processo Castellano* (1411-

Siena. House of Saint Catherine. *Painting realised in 1630 by the Siennese Rutilio Manetti for the Confraternity of Saint Catherine.*

1416) Caffarini could give testimony in the following words: *"when I was in Siena at the time of the epidemic, I saw Catherine visiting very many times the plague-stricken; and also I saw the joy with which she nursed the infected and likewise I witnessed how some of them miraculously getting cured from the plague and from other sicknesses because of her"*.

In autumn 1374 Catherine, along with Friar Raymond, went twice to the Monastery of Montepuliciano, founded by the first Dominican Saint, Agnes Segni (1268-1317), in 1299.

The following year was particularly a busy year for Catherine with full of important events: journeys of peace, meeting

Siena. House of Saint Catherine.
The Crucifix in front which Catherine received the stigmata on 1 April 1375. According to a tradition the precious image of the school of Pisana may have been donated by an Archbishop of Pisa to the city of Siena.

with political and religious leaders, intensive correspondence. It was also the year of stigmata which she received at Pisa in the Church of Santa Maria della Spina.

In this circumstance Raymond, Thomas della Fonte, Alessia Saracini, sister-in-law Lisa and the seventy year old Lapa were with her. The travelling group stayed in a house on the river bank of Arno, belonging to the noble Gherardo Buonconti. From this house she dictated many letters to those who were able to contribute to the "holy passage" - a term with which she called the Crusade.

But the news that she received from her native city was worrying. The notorious group of Giovanni Hawkwood, which had terrorised the city of Florence in the month of June, was now heading towards Siena. She did not hesitate to send Friar Raymond to meet the feared-captain in order to ask him to desist and to become a crusader. As a credential, she sent him a letter.

Her return to Siena, welcomed by her disciples with great joy, was providential particularly to the Perugine Niccolò of Tuldo, a young man condemned to death by the governors of the city.

At the Venice trial Caffarini bore witness by saying that the unlucky youngman, "*having fallen in the abyss of despair, was staying in prison like a ferocious lion*". But before he would be taken around the city on a cart, Catherine wanted to see him. The dramatic and sweet meeting was related by her in a splendid letter to Raymond: "*I went to visit him whom you know: when he received such comfort and consolation that he confessed, and prepared himself very well. And he made me promise by the love of God that when the time of the sentence should come, I would be*

Florence. Church of Santa Maria Novella.
In 1246 the Dominican Friars began the construction of the current Church. Its important portions were completed only in 1360.

Siena. Basilica of Saint Dominic.
Chapel of Saint Catherine. The fresco represents the dramatic beheading of Niccolò di Tuldo.

with him (…). I waited for him then at the place of justice (…). Then he came, like a gentle lamb; and seeing me, he began to smile, and wanted me to make the sign of the Cross. When he had received the sign, I said: "Down! To the Bridal, sweetest my brother! For soon you shall be in the enduring life." He prostrated himself with great gentleness, and I stretched out his neck; and bowed me down, and recalled to him the Blood of the Lamb. His lips said nothing but save

Jesus! and, Catherine! And so saying, I received his head in my hands".

Caffarini, who was present at the scene, bore witness at the trial: *"all those present cried and later declared of having seen not the execution of a culprit, but of a martyr".* In August 1375 Catherine once again left Siena in order to go to Lucca, where there was a sign of the city joining the antipapal league organised by Florence. Her rigorous political action on those responsible in the city had initial success. But, after her departure, she came to know that the politics of Lucca was once again working in favour of Florence.

Till the end of 1375, Catherine used all her diplomatic ability to disentangle the complicated situation of the political relationship between Pisa, Lucca, Florence and the Pope.

In January 1376 at Pisa she received the visit of Raymond and Friar Pietro of Velletri who brought the news about the insurgence of Perugia, now fallen in the hands of the enemies of the Pope. Seeing the friends very much afflicted because of the situation, Catherine told them: *"What you see today is all smiles compared to what is yet to happen. A kind of schism will happen in the Church and in the whole Christendom. Therefore, be prepared for this suffering".* In the meantime Pisa entered into league against the Pope, followed by Lucca, Urbino, Todi, Città di Castello, Gubbio and Forlì.

The gravity of the Italian political situation and of the Pontifical State had forced Catherine to send first of the fourteen letters to the Pope, Gregory XI, residing in Avignon. The invitation to return to Rome and to join the crusade was griefstricken: *"Press on, and fulfil with true zeal what you have begun with a holy resolve, con-*

Siena. Basilica of Saint Dominic. *Beheading of Niccolò di Tuldo. Details of the fresco.*

cerning your return, and the holy and sweet crusade. Pardon me, Father, that I have said so many words to you. You know that through the abundance of the heart the mouth speaks".

Catherine approached the supreme authority of the Church with vigorousness and almost authoritatively. She knew well what must be said and she said it with evangelical frankness, making also a reference to the consistory of 20th December 1375, during which Gregory XI appointed seven French Cardinals, an Italian and a Spaniard. Of the seven French Cardinals, three of them were his own relatives. According to Catherine this choice was one of the main obstacles for the return of the Pope to "*loco suo*", that is Rome. And again another time, she did not have any fear to reproach him: "*I have heard here that you have appointed the cardinals. I believe that it would honour God and profit us more if you would take heed always to appoint virtuous men. If the contrary is done, it will be a great insult to God, and disaster to Holy Church. Let us not wonder later if God sends us His disciplines and scourges; for the thing is just. I beg you to do what you have to do manfully and in the fear of God".*

Siena. Basilica of Saint Dominic.
Chapel of Saint Catherine. Details of the "fainting".

Towards Avignon

The proselytising act of Florence to make the neighbouring republics to join the League against the Pope was growing ever stronger. Following this, in February 1376 Gregory XI asked the Florentines to send the leaders of the city to him at Avignon – the city where the Popes resided from 1309. Donato Barbadori, Alessandro d'Antella and Domenico di Silvestro were sent there as ambassadors. As soon as they reached the place, they told the Pope that the leaders, whom he had asked to come, were unable to do so, because they were in prison. This way, instead of getting settled, the problem started worsening.

On 31 May the Pope responded Florence by hitting it back with an Interdict and by excommunicating the *Eight of War* (a new body of magistrates) as leaders of the rebellion and other fifty-one authoritative citizens, among them was Niccolò Soderini. It was then the Florentines understood that to get out of the deadlock, in which they were all caught, they had to make peace with the Pope. To do this, the only mediation that they could think of, was Catherine.

Having accepted the difficult job of peace mediator, Catherine sent Friar Raymond and other Dominicans, first of all to Avignon, with a new letter in which she invited the Pope to work on three fronts: to expel the unworthy priests from their offices; to bring back the Holy See to Rome, and initiate Crusade. At the end of May 1376 she herself went to Avignon accompanied by some twenty of her disciples.

**Avignon.
Palace of the
Popes**
(details).

Avignon. Palace of the Popes.
It was built in about thirty years (1334-1362), during the pontificates of Benedict XI, Clement VI and Innocent VI.

The work was not easy also because, as she came to know later on, the new leaders of Florence, following the *Eight of War*, had adopted policies against the Pope and had invited the European counterparts to join the Anti-Papal League.

Saddened because of the failure but not discouraged, Catherine dedicated all her energies in favour of the three great causes already recommended to the Pope.

The Pope listened to Catherine willingly, but the "palace" showed diffidence. The perplexity regarding her was spread not only among the twenty six cardinals (twenty-one Frenchmen, four Italians and one Spaniard), but also to other areas of Avignon. Three theologians, for example, asked the Pope for authorisation in order to examine the doctrinal orthodoxy of Catherine and the authenticity of her visions and the other mystical phenomena. But at the end of the rigorous interrogation, lasting a whole day, they gave up. They became Catherine's fervent defenders and friends.

Avignon. Palace of the Popes.
The mighty castle (15,000 square meters) has the look of a fortress: very high walls with narrow slits and windows, big pointed arcades, watch and defence towers.

*In this hall,
namely,
"Grandi
udienze", the
ecclesiastical
judges used to
gather
themselves.
Here on 20
June 1376
Catherine was
received by
Gregory XI for
the first time.*

The persistent requests of Catherine asking the Pope Gregory to leave Avignon made him perplexed. The reasons that she adopted were unexceptional, but her heart hesitated. After all, France was his land. Catherine intuited this and so not being able to have frequent dialogues, she had to have recourse to letters. In the period of July-September she sent him four letters: not long ones, but historically and from church point of view they were of great values.

Finally came the moment for Gregory to put into practice the *holy cheating* suggested by Catherine. Towards the beginning of September, without the knowledge of the Cardinals, Gregory got some flat-ships docked near the port of Marseilles.

The dream of many was becoming true. Certainly, it was not just because of Catherine's efforts alone, but without her it would have remained as it was.

Return to Rome

On 13 September 1376 Gregorio XI left the threshold of papal palace of Avignon for a journey without return.

Also Catherine left the city after receiving from the Pope some money for the journey. After a stop over at Tolone, she, along with her spiritual family, reached by sea the city of Varazze in Liguria on 3 October. The following day she arrived in Genoa where, because of the illness of some of her disciples, she was forced to stay for about a month longer. This long stay in the hospitable house of Monna Orietta Scotti was providential, because Catherine got a way to meet the Pope *en route* to Rome.

Gregory and the entire Roman curia reached Genoa on 18 October. Having heard that Rome was again in turmoil, and that the Florentines were fighting with success against the papal troops, he was on the verge of going back. Catherine intervened once again in order to strengthen the decision of Gregory to proceed to Rome. She did it efficiently in a secret dialogue at Scotti Palace. Corroborated by the words of Catherine, Gregory resumed his sea journey without hesitation, and on 5 December 1376 he finally disembarked at Corneto, the actual Tarquinia.

Rome. *Monument of Saint Catherine at the Castle Sant'Angelo (Francesco Messina, 1960).*

Siena. Fort of Saint Barbara.
From foot of the Fortress of Siena Saint Catherine blesses her city. The modern bronze statue is of Bruno Buracchini (1970).

Here he received a fresh letter from Catherine, who, in the meantime, had arrived at Siena. The city was all up against the Pontiff along with Florence, Perugia and Bologna. Catherine did not deny the wrongdoing of her city-people; she asked the Pope to excuse them for they had agitated out of necessity: *"Peace, peace, Holy Father! Let your Sanctity be pleased to receive your sons who have offended you. Let your benignity conquer their malice and pride. It will not be a shameful thing for you to become more humble in order to save the estranged son; instead, it would be for you a great honour and benefit in the sight of God and of the people of this world. Oh, Father, no more war for any reason whatsoever"*.

On 17 January 1377 Gregory XI finally entered Rome and was received with an understandable enthusiasm. But his escort looked too much bellicose in the eyes of Catherine, who had suggested to him not to go *"with pomp of people, but the cross in hand, like a docile lamb"*.

Catherine finally saw a dream being realised. The Pope returned to that Rome which St. Peter, in the words of Dante, had called *"il loco mio"* and that she, in a letter to the same Gregory, had defined *"the place of your predecessor and champion apostle Peter"*.

Rome.
Monument at Castle Sant'Angelo. Episode of life of the Saint (Francesco Messina, 1960).

Reconciler
in Val d'Orcia

Val d'Orcia. Rocca di Tentennano. *In 1274 the castle was handed over to Sennese family Salimbeni. For the whole period of 13th century, this was made into a main base of their stronghold.*

In 1377, after returning from Avignon to Siena, Catherine dedicated herself to founding a monastery for a community of Dominican nuns. She chose a castle situated a few kilometres from the city. It belonged to Nanni of ser Vanni Savini, a very well known person in Siena. The inauguration was had in the same year, with the authorisation of Pope Gregory. Thus the antique manor-house becomes a monastery for women with the name of Santa Maria degli Angeli.

When, however, the news about the atrocities committed by the militias of Hawkhood at Cesena reached Catherine, she could not be silent. A passionate letter of request for peace was dictated by her and was sent to the Pope. From Belcaro, on 9 April 1377 she wrote also to the prisoners of Siena calling them "*dearest sons in sweet Jesus Christ*". In her letter there was neither a word of condemnation nor a mention of their misdemeanour, but only an invitation to patience and conversion.

Besides helping people, those near and far, to get reconciled, Catherine did also deeds of liberation from devil, so much so people were coming to her, from villages and cottages of Val d'Orcia, with problems or demoniac subjugations.

She brought reconciliation also to Rocca di Tentennano in this valley. Two worst enemies of the family of Salimbeni, namely, Cione and Giovanni d'Agnolino made peace. Her fame, thus, spread all

Siena. House of Saint Catherine.
The painting of Pietro Sorri representing the Saint in the act of liberating a demoniac.

Abbey of Saint Antimo.
The antique abbey of Saint Antimo of the XII century, isolated in the quiet countryside near Montalcino.

the more widely. There was no problem that was not submitted to her discernment and there was no sick person who was not brought before her.

During the four months of stay in the valley – from the end of summer to the middle of December 1377 – she went to the abbey of Saint Antimo situated a few kilometres from Rocca dei Salimbeni: also this time the purpose was one of bringing peace.

It was during this period that Catherine, almost suddenly, learned to write. The first letter written by her was for Stefano Maconi, but unfortunately it did not reach him. We come to know this from Caffarini who, at the "Process", revealed that Maconi himself had told him of this.

However, the reconciliation mission in Val d'Orcia did not spare her from the problems that were afflicting the temporary government of Gregory XI.

Thus in November 1377 she felt the need of still writing to him.

Mission in Florence

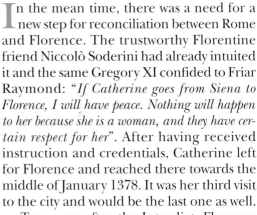

Illustration of the Siennese Lorenzo of Pietro (1480) preserved in the National Pinacoteque of Siena.

In the mean time, there was a need for a new step for reconciliation between Rome and Florence. The trustworthy Florentine friend Niccolò Soderini had already intuited it and the same Gregory XI confided to Friar Raymond: *"If Catherine goes from Siena to Florence, I will have peace. Nothing will happen to her because she is a woman, and they have certain respect for her"*. After having received instruction and credentials, Catherine left for Florence and reached there towards the middle of January 1378. It was her third visit to the city and would be the last one as well.

Two years after the Interdict, Florence was plunging into disastrous economic problems. The social and political conditions were not either better due to the fighting-factions in the society. With her visit, Catherine wanted to arrive at two things: to convince the city about the observance of the punishment given by the Pope and to make the people to agree with the Pontiff.

Having been received with great respect, she immediately started to work. With the providential mediation of Niccolò Soderini, she managed to meet some authoritative citizens at Palazzo Vecchio to whom she extended an urgent invitation to make peace with the Pontiff. Then she had dialogue with the political leaders of the Guelphs and asked them to dismiss all those who wanted to impede the peace process with the Pope because, she said: *"they were not to be called as agitators, but destroyers of the common good and of the city"*.

The measures taken by the governing body were but different. Their 'admonitions' – the deliberations with which they hampered the Ghibellines' power access or expelled the undeserving from government offices - became in fact occasions for personal vendetta.

On 22 June 1378 the fighting between the factions reached at a maximum level with the so-called 'tumult of the Ciompi'; all poor wool-teasers, like many other penniless people, had to remain at the margin of social life. The city was ravaged by anarchy and terror for days. None seemed to be able to stem the violence and bring the angry crowd to its senses. The rebels shouted: *"Down the hypocrite Niccolò and her saint Catherine"*.

According to Friar Raymond, Catherine and her friends were in grave danger. None was willing to give them hospitality. But whoever advised her to get back to Siena, she replied right away saying she could not do so, until peace was made with the Pope. This was the responsibility received and this had to be fulfilled. The search for finding a secure place finally resulted positive. Her little group of "caterinati" (disciples) now could move into a safer place. Probably, it was the monastery of the Camaldian monks at Vallombrosa.

In the month of August she returned to Siena where she completed the *Dialgoue* – a sublime treatise on asceticism and mysticism which almost constitutes the spiritual testament for her disciples. Catherine dictated the book to her

The miniature reproduces the first page of the law "Libellus de Supplemento" of Friar Tommasso da Siena.

usual secretary disciples (Barduccio Canigiani, Stefano Maconi, Neri di Landoccio), while she was in ecstasy.

While being in ecstasy she used to pray and ask. Since prayers and supplications were born not from abstract thinking, but from concrete life situations – personal, social, political and ecclesial – the entire book is characterised by a vigorous recording of history. This is the book's great peculiarity. The topics are not dealt with in an organic way, but their content, which is rich in doctrine, makes reference to other classical phases of spiritual life (purification, illumination, union), called, imperfect stage, perfect stage, and the most perfect stage, respectively.

Saint Catherine of Siena. A fresco realised by the painter Bernardino de' Rossi (1450-1514) in a small church at Pavia.

The Exodus

With the return of the Holy See to Rome many had believed that the major part of the problems of the Church would be resolved. But it was not so. Instead, the worst was yet to come: the Great Western Schism.

On 27 March 1378 Gregory XI died and his successor Urban VI had to face those, who nostalgic of Avignon, elected an antipope Clement VII in a "contro-conclave". This antipope quickly brought back the Holy See to the French city. This way, after the Eastern Schism of 1054, the Western Schism happened and ended in 1417 after 39 years.

From August 1378 onwards Catherine worked tirelessly in order to affirm the validity of the election of Urban VI. She knew that the pretext for the schism was the rejection of the reform that he wanted to bring about into the life of the Church. She wrote letters to Cardinals, to Queen Giovanna of Naples, to the King of Hungary.

Pope Urban VI, who by then had received another letter from Catherine,

Siena. Basilica of Saint Dominic. *A modern representation of Saint Catherine.*

wanted to speak to her and she, without hesitation, came to him in 1378. The Pope asked her to convince the Queen Giovanna of Naples to back down from supporting the schism. But he wanted her not to go alone to that corrupt palace, but along with the princess Catherine of Wadstena, daughter of saint Briget of Sweden (1302-1373), who was in Rome to promote her mother's canonization.

Due to various reasons the journey did not take place, even though Catherine stayed in Rome. The house of Via Santa Chiara, in which she was staying in the company of many people, among them her mother Lapa, was not far from the convent of Santa Maria above Minerva where Raymond served as its prior. Like in many other places, she found bitterness also in Rome. One such instance was the departure of Friar Raymond – December 1378 – who, as legate of Urban VI, was about to go to France taking with him a difficult task of making the King Charles to withdraw support for the schism. After the departure of Raymond, Catherine dedicated herself fully for the realisation of other two great dreams: the unification of the Church and the Crusade for the liberation of the Holy Land.

The Lent of 1379 was a fervent time of prayer for Catherine. Twelve years earlier, on 'Shrove Tuesday' 1367 she had celebrated the mystical weddings with Jesus in the house of Fonte Branda. To Him she now said prayers that were later on written down by her disciples.

The evening of 30 January 1380, she had a serious crisis. It was the beginning of rapid worsening of her health which was to bring her death, after a few months.

Siena.

Steeple and bell tower of the cathedral church.

More than her sufferings, Catherine worried about the problems of the Church. She gathered strength to dictate a letter for Urban VI which Barduccio Canigiani figured out from her faint voice. With this she asked the Pope to have more benevolence and love towards the enemies because she said: *"People are drawn and held more with gentleness than with any force or asperity of words; Remain. Remain in the holy and sweet Grace of God. Humbly I ask your benediction. Sweet Jesus, Jesus Love."*

On 15 February 1380, by then at the end of her life, Catherine sent a final letter to Friar Raymond, written by her own hand, and with which she asked pardon: *"And I beg you that you pardon me every disobedience, irreverence, and ingratitude which I*

Siena, House of Saint Catherine.
The fresco of Girolamo of the Pacchia symbolizes the stigmatization of Catherine (1525).

**Pienza.
Cathedral.**
*Details of
tempera on
panel
representing
the Assumption
of the Virgin
among the
Angels and the
Saints realised
in 1461 by
Lorenzo di
Pietro, called
"il Vecchietta".*

showed to you or committed against you, and all pain and bitterness which I may have caused you: and the slight zeal which I have had for our salvation. And I ask you for your blessing". More than being a letter, the writing seems to be the testament of Catherine, wherein the initial narration of the indescribable sufferings, both in body and spirit, is gradually seen in the remembrance of people dear to her and in the request for pardon and prayer.

From the beginning of February to the middle of March of the final year of life, it was impossible for her to move from the bed. However Caffarini wrote: *"Never ever escaped a word of grumbling from her lips, but she used to say that what she was enduring was a small thing".*

In the night before 29 April 1380, her *dies natalis*, Catherine received the Sacraments of Reconciliation and of the Sick. She asked also for the Plenary Indulgence *in articulo mortis.* During the last moments of her agony, the disciples who were staying closer to her, heard her pronouncing almost enigmatic words: *"Vain glory no, but the true glory and praise of God, yes".*

It was about 12 o'clock on Sunday 29 April 1380. She lived only 33 years and 35 days. She had loved Christ above all things, she had imitated Him in death and now she could contemplate Him in fullness of light.

A few months later, on 8 September 1380, another famous saint, Bernardino da Siena, her co-citizen by adoption, was born in the near by village of Massa Marittima. And the following year, as if to mark the continuity of spiritual importance, the most venerated Rita of Cascia was born in a mountain village in the neighbouring Umbria.

The Glorification

In the morning on 30 April 1380 the remains of Catherine was brought to the near by Dominican church of Saint Mary above Minerva. The death news spread rapidly all over Rome and people came in huge numbers. Friar Giovanni Tantucci, the confessor of Catherine, who celebrated the funeral rites, said just this: *"I had planned to say a few things in order to commemorate this virgin saint but, as it is known to all, she does not need our preaching, because her Bridegroom Himself is honouring her"*.

Immediately after this, a series of extraordinary cures started to take place, some of which were described by Raymond basing on documents and direct testimonies. Likewise the diaspora of disciples also started to grow. Each one followed his/her proper vocation, often explicitly indicated by their teacher. Although the roads were different, the spiritual heritage that they carried in their hearts and the commitments in favour of two specific objectives remained identical: service to the Church in crisis because of the schism, and the canonisation of their "mamma".

This took place at the end of the ritual of canonical process which was celebrated in Venice from 24 May 1411 to 20 July 1416. It was the Siennese, Pius II (1458-1464), the well-known humanist Enea Silvio Piccolomini, who elevated the noblest daughter of his city to glory. Again it was he who gave the discourse on the heroic theological virtues of Catherine and to

Siena. Basilica of Saint Dominic.
Raymond of Capua, in the act of writing the Legenda Maior. Fresco by the Siennese artist Francesco Vanni (1563-1610) on the left arch of the Chapel of Saint Catherine.

In ȝpi nomine amen anno natiuitatis eiusdem
millesimoquadringentesimo vndecimo indictione
quarta die vigesimoquarto mensis maij. Ad
ppetuam rei memoriam pateat cuibȝ infrascripta
legentibȝ. Et cum magno tpre in couentu
sanctoȝ Johannis et pauli sancti dominici ac
in menasterio corporis ȝpi de Venetijs ordinis
friũ pdicatoȝ celebrata fuerit memoria cuidã
Virginis bte kateruie de senis in diñca videlicet
que sequit imediate festum bñ Petri martiris ordinis pdicatoȝ.
Contingit anno pdicto qr cum memoria pdca in dicto couentu scõ
Johannis et pauli celebraret more et tempore solito, et pdica
ret ibidem ille qui tñc erat pdicator dei couentus videlȝ quidã
Venerabilis pater frater Bertholameus de feiraua ortum est
quoddam murmur inter aliquos dicte Virginis aliquali detrahetes
ex grandi admiratione lacta de virtutibȝ eximijs que dicebant de
illa et aliquos alios ȝpi Virginis non pura deuotioe affectos. Ex
quo secutum est ut p quosdam discretos viros ordiatis exhtit qr
apud dñm epñm Castellani fiet quedã querella sup pdca ña Vt
ipe dñs epñs hijs aliquibȝ iformatoribȝ aliquȝ prium supdicti

read the Bull of Canonisation *Misericordias Domini*, written personally by him.

It was on the 29 June 1461.

114 years elapsed between the day of "transito" and that of the glorification – Catherine was the only woman to be canonised in the Fourteenth century.

On 4 October 1970 Paul VI proclaimed her "doctor of the universal Church", a title till then was given only to some thirty great men theologians and a woman, Therese of Avila.

This prestigious "laureate" of theology given to a commoner, who spent most of her younger days doing domestic works and, still worse, was an illiterate, can be surprising. But the piety, devotion and the art itself, which symbolises her often in the act of dictating texts or giving them to disciples, had preceded the formal recognition of Paul VI.

In the previous page:
Castellano Process.
The first page of the manuscript goes back to the first half of the XV century.

Rome. Basilica of Saint Mary above Minerva.
The sarcophagus of Saint Catherine has been enclosed in a precious cell in front of the main altar.

Rome. Basilica of Saint Mary above Minerva.

The inside of this church, with nave and single aisle, was begun in 1280. On 9 August 1855, inaugural day of the renovated temple, the sarcophagus of Saint Catherine was moved to the front side of the main altar.

Indice